A TOY BLACK SOLDIERS STORY

A TOY BLACK SOLDIERS STORY

SGT. JAMES R. WILLIS

ARPress
ILLUMINATING IDEAS.
EMPOWERING VOICES

ARPress
45 Dan Road Suite 5
Canton MA 02021
Hotline: 1(888) 821-0229
Fax: 1(508) 545-7580

Ordering Information:
Quantity sales. Special discounts are available on quantity purchases by corporations, associations, and others. For details, contact the publisher at the address above.

Printed in the United States of America.

ISBN-13:   Paperback   979-8-89389-793-7
           eBook   979-8-89389-794-4

Library of Congress Control Number: 2024923296

DEDICATION

To everything there is a season, and a time to every purpose under the heaven. A time to be born, and a time to die, a time to plant, and a time to pluck up that which is planted. A time to kill, and a time to heal, a time to break down, and a time to build up, a time to weep, and a time to laugh; a time to mourn, and a time to dance, a time to cast away stones, and a time to gather stones together, a time to embrace, and a time to refrain from embracing. A time to get, and a time to lose, a time to keep, and a time to cast away. A time to end, and a time to sew; a time to keep silence, and a time to speak. A time to love, and a time to hate, a time of war, and a time of peace. I have seen the travail, which God hath given to the sons of men to exercise in it. He hath made to everything beauty but in his time and I know there is no good in it but to rejoice and to do good in life.

A TOY BLACK SOLDIERS STORY

Coming from Cabrini Green Projects in June 1966, this all seems like a dream to a young high school graduate of Tilden Technical High School on the South Side of Chicago, who commuted back and forth on a bus from the North Side of Chicago to the South Side for four years to get an education outside of the ghetto. At home my mother and father were struggling to raise ten children at wages below national average in the country. There was hope in my mother's eyes that her children would escape the nightmare of poverty and shame. She said we could be anything we wanted because God's grace was upon us and that we were born to be successful even though our position in the projects looked hopeless. Three brothers tried to form a band at home in the projects and the five girls were good in school. The oldest and the second to oldest competed to be gr#eat against each other. My father was a forgotten hero who served under general Wainwright in World War II and was lost in the Philippine Conflict for three years fighting hand to hand with the Japanese. This obstacle had hindered him and haunted his progress in life due to war torn memories, which led to a life of hardship and struggle the care of his children. He was still loved by all of us because he was a hero. My father worked as a security guard and always wanted to be a Chicago police officer. In his heart his service for his country during World War II as a soldier gallantly was never forgotten. Once I asked what it was like to be left behind and cut off by the enemy on an island filled with Japanese soldiers for three long years and why did mom wait for him under such impossible circumstances? He told me about missions that he volunteered to rescue American prisoners from the death march on the island held by the Japanese. And how impossible missions were undertaken to steal food from Japanese camps in the middle of the night so the Left behind American troops could survive while hiding in the mountains and caves of the island. On one occasion, while talking about his part in front of my mother and I, my father stated that in the middle of the night he volunteered to sneak into a Japanese camp and steal food to bring back to American survivors. They were discovered and he remembered the shooting and his running towards the hills for safety in tile dark. He stated that it felt like a stream that he was running through in the dark because water was up to his knees. He said the next morning orders were given by the commander to go down the side of the hill and rescue the soldiers who were wounded, still alive, or. lost. As he went down the hill, a river of blood flowed past him and he realized all these Americans were killed in the dark from the mission that he undertook, and what he then thought was a stream was actually blood he was running through. I looked at my mother and asked her why you would wait on someone in such an impossible situation? My father looked at her in suspense for the answer to my question. She responded by the gleam in her eyes and I knew the answer. He was her hero. This changed my outlook about what I would do after high school. I was in Chicago's second best academic high school and I was in the upper 10 percent of my class. Dreams were that I would be a lawyer or senator from my father. My mother thought I'd be a doctor like my second brother decided to be. But my parents had no finances to send me to college and I was not factory material or US Postal Service Mail Handler material. These were jobs available for high school graduates during my time. I talked to the military recruiters and decided if I volunteer a future would be available after I got out of my military service. Benefits would be there for education and other needs such as hospital care, housing, and trades. It was the Vietnam war, and mostly everyone was being drafted who were not working or in school. The Cabrini Green Projects sons were being cleared out. Even Tilden Tech High School students had suffered some of my classmates to the draft. We were hearing reports of deaths in Vietnam daily from high school and neighborhood friends but I volunteered anyway. This was a terrible time, and explaining this to my religious mother and grandmother was not going to be easy. I was an athlete in high school and was the on the best wrestling team in the state and was an outstanding baseball player. These sports came naturally to me and I was all-city and all-state as a player. I was interviewed by the Chicago Cubs and the Los Angeles Dodgers but I had made up my mind to serve my country. I told my parents of my decision. The day that I was leaving for basic training. My mother went into her room and cried. She said why you? My father just stood there and said nothing. I went to my room and packed and when I ran down the stairs to leave, he stood at the door with a smile and saluted. I told him to tell my mom I will see her and that she will always be my best girl, my brothers and sisters were asleep in their rooms. The army induction center at Van Buren and Canal Street was packed. Everything was hurry up and wait! Physical and quick psychological exams were given all day, and buses took loads of people away all day long. I remember Diana Ross coming across the radio with her song "Love is Here and Now You're Gone," and it brought memories of my popularity in high school and my girlfriend Shirley. I would marry her once I got settled in the base camp. Little did I know, the song by Diana Ross would be the last memory of Shirley. I heard a loud call to saddle up and get in line, all new recruits and we were taken into a room in front of two large American flags. A captain came out and some other officers and said stand at attention and raise your right hand. The oath of allegiance was stated and we were sent to the buses for departure. Some kids were crying and some were in shock. I turned to a kid and said why are you crying? He said he didn't want to go to Vietnam and die. He was drafted, I told him that I volunteered, and he said why? Several others in the line came to a standstill and were awaiting my answer. I said this is the way to victory and glory. They didn't understand.

Once on the bus, I began to wonder where my best friend Booker was and my other friend Floyd. I knew Booker was drafted and that maybe I would see him somewhere, Floyd was a high school dropout and the son of a father spending life in prison for drugs. His mother died of an overdose and his grandmother was raising him and his brother. He never had structure, and he followed me from the third grade until we separated at high school age. We were close. I wondered what would happen to him now that I was gone. What would become of my brothers and sisters? Little did I know that while serving in Vietnam, I would get a letter from home that said Floyd was sent to prison for 35 years on a robbery charge and was stabbed 35 times and thrown over a prison deck to his death. My best friend Booker, son of a prominent preacher, would be wounded in the shoulder and leg during an assault with the 1st Calvary division in operation Sam Houston 4/1968 and sent back home with mangled body parts decorated with a bronze star and purple heart to die in the streets of Chicago. He was full of drugs and alcohol and out of his mind when he fell dead in an alley behind Cabrini Green projects.

The bus ride ended and we were here at basic training camp. Shouting and orders were all over the place. The drill instructors were in your face every minute. I noticed a sign that read "Be all that you can be" and the big flag in the middle of the post as a tough sergeant hauled us new recruits away to a tent. We were placed in our bunk areas and either stood at attention or marched from that moment on everywhere we went. On the second day at 4:00 AM, a whistle blew, and three sergeants came into the tent yelling get out of those beds, do it now! We were ordered to dress and march in single file toward some large tent. I saw a mountain of potatoes and I asked the recruit in front of me what was going on, as if he knew. He said I think we are going into that tent to peel those potatoes. I said, not me. The sergeant overheard our conversation and got in my face saying what are you talking about? Don't you talk neighbors son who had been taken away in the draft by military force while trying to hide in another apartment on an upper floor of the building. He was a star basketball player in high school with a promising future and wanted to play professional basketball. Everyone was talking about how he hated the war and felt no black man owed anything to the Unites States since we got nothing but misery from it. A few friends were talking about my being home on leave and the neighbors all around wanted to see me. It seems all I heard were stories of their sons being killed or wounded in the war and I was the talk of the neighborhood since it was my tum to serve. I avoided crowds and tried to hide behind sunglasses. Going to places I would not be seen while in the neighborhood. A visit to my old high school was pleasant. Several teachers came out of the classroom to see me while I visited. The history and math teachers bragged about my exceptional performance in their classes. The wrestling coach and baseball coach cried, My picture was hanging in the school entrance as a memorial to those who hailed the halls of Tilden and would never be forgotten. Many kids wanted to know how I felt about going to Vietnam. I avoided some and the ones I could not avoid I simply stated that it was my duty to serve and I would do it proudly. In the house my brothers and father were practicing with the band 'Soulful Generation" as it was called profusely in my old room. They wanted to treat me like royalty at home and offered me my parents' room. I refused the room by saying that I would be staying at my cousins house since he was upset at having been drafted while I was away and was thinking about running away to avoid duties in Vietnam. We were close growing up and I remembered how he tried to compete in every area of sports to outdo me in high school. He was all-city in wrestling and tried to be a basketball star in high school but was too short. He was a good boxer and made it to the junior Olympics during his senior year at Cooley high school. Andrew left for basic training with my advice before my leave was over. This was the last time I would see him alive. He was killed in a place called Bien Hua, Vietnam during a tet offensive in 1969.

My leave seemed to rapidly disappear and I spent the last two days at home with my family. Back in my old room the band was silent and everyone stayed quiet about me leaving. I would accept no calls from the many friend and neighbors trying to call to wish me well or to tell me how sad they were about my having to go to Vietnam. My door was always shut to my room and I didn't pull pranks or jokes on my brothers and sisters as I once did. I remember one of my favorite pranks was done when a celebrity visited Chicago back during my sophomore year in high school had given me a ventriloquist doll. One evening at home I brought it to the kitchen table unannounced and sit it in my sisters chair at the table. My mother came home and said "What is that!" I answered through the doll. She thought I had gone crazy and said get that doll away from the table. All the other family members except my father came running to the kitchen to see what was going on. Everyone was laughing and rolling around on the floor and furniture in tears of laughter. My mother called my dad at work and said he needed to come home and take me to the hospital. When my dad arrived home he saw me sitting at the table with the doll and just stared. He finally said come into my parents' bedroom so he could talk to me. I tried to bring the doll with me but he said leave it outside. "the doll said I aint goin' nowhere but with him." Dad said I don't know what this is all about but your mother wants me to take you to the hospital. He said are you sick? The doll said, "Only of the school lunch." Dad said here is five dollars son and left the bedroom and went back to work. He never said another word about that doll. It was sitting on the chair where I left it prior to leaving for the military. I wondered why Shirley hadn't called since we were high school sweethearts and seemed to avoid me in the neighborhood. I called her mother and she stated that she didn't know what's wrong with her and I asked her why you don't talk to him but Shirley would not answer he mother. I didn't press the issue. The last night at home all kinds of crazy thoughts ran though my mind. Why didn't I go on to pursue a baseball career? Why didn't I go to junior college until I got a scholarship and why did I break my family's heart? It was late in the evening when a knock occurred on my bedroom door and house had gone quiet with all the family members in the living room watching the family programs. At first I didn't know whether to open the door or not. My mother called out my name and I opened the door. She came into my room and sat on the bed next to me and said to me I know you are worried about Vietnam but nothing will happen to you. I want you to stop worrying and be the son I know you are. My mother had the same glean in her eyes that I saw when she looked at my father the day he told us his story about actions performed by him in the Philippines during World War II. The second hero was in the home. She went out of the room and looked back with a smile as she closed the door. I was up early and tried to leave while everyone was asleep but as I quietly left my room and made it to the front door my father was waiting for me. He came to the door and he said you are my son and I will always be proud of you no matter what you do.

We hugged and I rushed out of the door and away to the bus stop. It was so early no neighbors saw me and there were only a few people on the bus. I hid behind my sunglasses to avoid being recognized and asked questions. At my point of departure the bus driver opened the door in the front instead of the back where I wanted to get off and I went up front to exit. As I was getting off he stood at attention and saluted me. This made me feel proud to be an American.

Departure and Entrance to Cam Rahn Bay, Vietnam was a living hell. There were young soldiers calling home for the last time at Seattle, Washington, in tears. Some were fearful and many just sat in silence waiting for the planes to take us to Vietnam. I wanted to call someone and thought of my sweetheart Shirley Ann, but I didn't call. It was my turn to saddle up and head for the "boonies" as it was called. The plane seemed to take forever getting off the runway and out of the United States. When on the way, the Battle Hymn of America played over the intercom along with When Johnnie Comes Marching Home. It was a silent trip and very few words were said during the flight by anyone. The plane tried to land in Cam Rhan Bay, Vietnam almost as if we were there in only a few moments from leaving Washington D. C. I realized the shock had lost sight of time on the way to Vietnam. Over the loud speaker came a voice saying the place was under attack and we would be circling the area until it was safe to land. Everyone was quiet and some of us wondered what was going on down below. We could not hear any gunfire and no one was shooting at the plane. The voice came back over the speaker and said saddle up and go. The plane never landed on the ground and we jumped from about four feet from the ground to the drop. Everyone was running toward a large building similar to O'Hare airport. It seemed we were all out and they was gone in seconds. I wondered where did he go so fast and why?

In the terminal military buses were available to all departure points in Vietnam we were assigned. The bus for Phan Kang came and I jumped on board. The trip was very strange to me a city boy. The roads were without sidewalks, there were mountains everywhere. Red mud seemed to be everywhere. Strange animals were all along the roadway and finally I saw people in black pajamas with funny looking straw hats in fields along the way. I asked a soldier who was on the bus to Phan Rang back from leave what kind of place this was. He said you'll find out. I asked him how long he had been there and he stated 30 days and a wake up. Later I found out that meant he was counting the days to go home as everyone did in Vietnam. The base at Phan Kang looked like something out of an old cowboy movie and the people seemed unreal. I reported to the command post and was greeted by a sergeant yelling out names and pointing to tents where we were to be assigned. When I entered my destination the guys stood up as I came in and said welcome to Vietnam, you'll be sorry. They all went back to doing what they were doing as I unpacked and settled into my bunk. A young soldier from Texas came over to my bunk and asked where I was from. We started talking about Chicago and his home of Houston, Texas. He told me that he had played in a band back home called Archie Bell and the Drills. He was a piano player and they had made a record called Tighten

Up. It was selling all over the country back home. We would become best of friends until he was killed in action. I can remember days when his popularity caused guys in the company to sit around the tent and listen to him play all night long. Sometimes he would be called on to travel around Vietnam to put on shows for other posts. Joel was a funny and compassionate guy who brought a ray of sunshine and hope to anyone he came across. He had a special talent and used it wisely. We were best of friends.

My first patrol in the bush as it was called sent us into the village on a good will mission. We passed out candy, bandages, and food to the civilians. None of them spoke English so the squad interpreter was speaking to them in Vietnamese. I seemed to get attention from the young children gathering around me wanting to play with me. Since I was a kid at heart we played kickball and I tried to teach them baseball. Their parents stared and looked in surprise at how the children seemed to be having fun with me. For a while it seemed as if there was no war. The doctor patched up several people and gave medicine to the sick. A voice yelled out to saddle up and lets go.

As we got back on the trucks I looked back at the kids I played with and was still trying to keep their attention by juggling a baseball in the air. The kids were laughing at me. Suddenly I heard shots in the background and all the people started pulling off their bandages and throwing the food and gifts in the air. I wondered what was going on. When we got back to the base I told some of the soldiers in my tent what had happened and asked why did they destroy the help we gave them. They said these people are Vietcong sympathizers and that they were afraid the Vietcong would come into the village after we were gone and kill them for taking gifts from us. I said what about the children, the answer was them too. I laid in my bunk wondering what kind of place had I come to. The days seemed to drag on and on with patrols, missions, and meaningless duties until one day I came back from patrol and found a crowd standing around the tent yelling and screaming at what appeared to be someone dressed in a white sheet on top of the tent reciting scenes from the Julius Caesar play. Suddenly he rolled off the top and on to the ground. He was dead. The young soldier had died of a drug overdose which he had taken because he couldn't live with the reality of being in Vietnam. There would be many more deaths around the base camp from drugs and alcohol before the year was over. I would suffer many unpleasant experiences over the time because of this problem.

In February 1969 it rained constantly day in and day out. Never had I seen rainfall or dreamed it could fall in this way. The camp was constantly under attack and it s,eemed we could not get sleep at all. You laid down and immediately there was an attack and you were sleeping while standing in a bunker. Finally the sun came out in April and I was back on patrol. I didn't spend a lot of time with my best friend Joel because we were on separate patrols all the time. The darkest day came when I had come back from a patrol and found out that the base camp had been under a fierce attack and that Joel had been hit by a rocket. Everyone was going crazy. I asked where he was and I was told down at the hospital tent. I ran down to the tent and so many wounded were lying on the tables with screams from lost limbs and dying, it was hard for me to find Joel. I saw him lying on a table with two big holes in his chest and doctors trying to resuscitate him. He looked up and recognized me and said we are going home together to race cars aren't we? Before I could answer, he went into shock and died. I ran from the tent and it seemed my whole life was going away and I could not bring it back. Nothing was the same after his death. I tried counting days before I could get out of this hellhole. Sometimes I would hang around the chaplain services or try to associate with the guy who had become numb to the war and just didn't care. Nothing seemed to help.

At last, my leave came of one week near the end of my tour. I chose Bangkok, Thailand for R & R, as it was called. This is when I met T.C., another Texas kid. We were going on R&R together. Both of us were excited about Thailand. We decided to be roommates at the hotel. The first night out was like being home. There were crowds of people like I had never seen before in the streets. So many people you could get lost just standing next to someone if you didn't keep your eye on them. We heard loud music every-were. Soldiers were in every place and bar. It was one big party. I went into a bar and saw girls that were carrying dolls that were as pretty as the dolls they were carrying. This was very different and strange to me. Most of them did not speak English and you had no way to find someone in the room to interpret for you if there was something you wanted from the bar. I liked the atmosphere and slipped back by myself in the second night. T.C. had found a girlfriend and was staying with her in the hotel. In the bar, I sat in the corner dreaming about going home and was lost from the reality of the events going on in the bar. Finally a woman who appeared to be a dignitary came over and asked me if I was having a good time in Thailand. I said, you speak English? She said of course. I asked her how did she learn and she stated that she was educated in the United States and came back home to set up this club. She was the owner. I lied and told her that everything was fine and that I was okay. Several girls came to the table and I sent them away. I believe that the owner had sent them but I was preoccupied with wanting to go home. The music seemed to be giving me a headache and I was ready to leave when a beautiful girl from behind the bar and just sat at the table next to me without any invitation. I looked at her and said what do you want? I'm leaving. She said why don't you give us a chance and enjoy yourself. I asked her if she speaks English, she said of course. I wanted to know how? And she stated that her mother was the owner of the bar and that she had went to school in England and France. She said I speak English, French, and Vietnamese. I told her I spoke French and English. I learned French in high school. She was a dream come true and I knew this was a magical relationship that was destined for love. We were an instant romance. She and I talked forever and it seemed the place was closed to us. I was in the corner with her so long until T.C. came to the bar looking for me. He said I was gone over 8 hours and he thought something had happened. He looked shocked that I was sitting so close with Lin and wondered what was going on. I said we've been together talking and I didn't realize the time. TC. said you have been gone for 8 hours have you been at this table all this time? T. C. was shocked that she spoke English and was so beautiful. I told him that she was the owner's daughter and we have a friendship. T.C. said "a romance" you mean. The three of us went back to the hotel and T.C.'s new girlfriend met us there. She had gone home to handle some chores and errands. It was amazing how Lin had so much in common with me. She was a great swimmer and loved all sports. Excitement was always happening around her and me. This was a romance that would remain in my heart for life. The R&R was ending and the day before I began to think about my relationship with Lin. I was in love and did not want to leave her behind. I decided not to return to Vietnam or Phan Rhang. I told T.C. that I was going to live with her in Thailand. He was unable to change my mind and said well if you are going to stay that he would too. So I went off with her to her family's house somewhere in the mountains of Thailand and way back there she introduced me to family members, at her mothers house it was the most gorgeous residence I have ever seen. It seemed like a king's castle and was contained with everything one could desire. They were wealthy beyond anything I had ever seen. In the yard were two of her cousins playing with what looked to be a Russian made handgun. I thought they were Vietcong and I was done. Lin talked to them in Vietnamese and they seemed to like me and acted as if I weren't in an American uniform. We went fishing and they let me use their boat to take her down the bay. Night came and I was lying in the room with Lin but couldn't sleep so I was pacing the floor and looking at how beautiful the city looked from this suburban residence. Everything was so peaceful and romantic. There was asleep the most beautiful girl I had ever seen. I was tom between duty and love. How was I going to make a decision like I had told T.C.? During the night I heard my mother's voice and I saw my brothers and sisters. I remembered the good times and the unfairness of being poor back in the United States. Staying with Lin seemed to be the right thing to do. I heard "When Johnny Comes Marching Home" playing and saw Joel dying again. This torture was giving me a struggle between heaven and hell. I saw the senselessness of the war and the racism back home. But in the military I saw a brotherhood and a family. Daylight came and I had fallen asleep. When I woke up Lin was gone. I began to panic and ran to the front of the house. Outside she was getting a cab to take us back to the city. I wonder if she knew that I was going back to Vietnam without me telling her. At the hotel she said I'll be back in a few hours, there was something her mother wanted her to do. I told T.C. we must go back to Vietnam and let's pack since leave was over. I waited for her but she never came. We got in a cab and went to the airport. Once the plane took off I reached in my pocket and found a picture signed by her that said "I'll love you forever, Goodbye, - Lin." It was a moment that will live forever in my heart. Back in Vietnam, the base camp suffered 68 attacks in one month. It was like living in a vacuum. I seemed to drift from the death of my closest friend back to the good times I had at home. On a Saturday afternoon, I went to town and while in the place it suddenly became off limits due to the Vietcong sneaking into it while we were off guard duty on the parameter. All the brothers were in one place and the whites in another. I guess after all the excitement an alarm was sounded over the loud speaker to return back to camp but I never heard it. TC was in the place and preoccupied with the girls. Suddenly a Vietnamese captain walked into the place with three other soldiers and started speaking in Vietnamese. I thought he was talking about my mother when he said "Do mami muk yea" or some garbage like that. I jumped up in his face and told him that I'd kick his ass and throw him into the streets and that I didn't care who was with him. The Vietnamese girls were afraid and he just stared at me and ordered his men to leave. I later learned on the base that he was saying I was under arrest as a prisoner of war and that he was going to transport TC and myself to North Vietnam. But I guess the captain had saw what war had done to me before I did. The war seemed to be someplace in the back of my dreams and I was going to wake up and it was going to be just another bad dream. Orders were coming in sending soldiers home everyday and I was getting closer to waking up. There was one last incident in which we were sent on patrol to a village as a hospitality group to provide medical care to young children as a way to gain support around keeping the Vietnamese on our side and against Vietcong sympathizers. The patrol was 10 clicks (known as miles) outside the base camp when suddenly I heard a click noise. The lead member of the team stepped on a Claymore Mine and I woke up in a hospital in Cam Rhan Bay Vietnam. The place was a nightmare. Screams from soldiers who had lost limbs, sight, and minds were all over the hospital complex. I thought that my limbs were gone or that I was dead. It was a horrible thought in my mind and I began to feel my body all over and found no missing parts. The nurse came into the room and saw I was awake. She said sergeant how are you? I didn't really know. The nurse told me that I suffered a blow to my helmet from shrapnel and was knocked unconscious. There were no other injuries. Nine of the men on patrol were dead and two were paralyzed from the waist down and had been evacuated back home. I was going to be sent home as well. Lying in bed I asked myself "for what?" over and over. When the colonel and his staff of officers came into the room to see us I waited for orders sending me home. I was told that home was just a few days away. It was really all over. But lying in the bed I though about Joel and TC as well as many others who were killed or wounded during this struggle for life and decided I would not go home, but continue to struggle with my remaining friends. They tried to force me back home but I was ready to refuse orders if I had to. The colonel and his staff just stared at me and said you can return to duty. Nothing seemed to matter anymore abou1 the war. I was just doing my job. Time seemed to hurry up at last and the next day seemed to find me on a plane heading back to the USA. The ride home was like going some place in a hearse. The plane didn't have many soldiers on it and there was little talking aboard. Music played through the loud speaker and suddenly Diana Ross was singing "Love is Here and Now You're Gone." My thoughts of Shirley came back to me and I wondered what my family was doing at the house. Once I landed at O'Hare airport in Chicago and went through the terminal I saw my father and younger brother at the gate waiting for me. Dad was smiling and had tears in his eyes. This was the first time I had ever seen him cry. He ran up to me and gave me a hug which seemed to last forever. I said hello dad I'm ok. My younger brother was excited about the medals on my shirt. There was silence in the car all the way home and I hid behind sunglasses and war torn memories. At the house, my mother ran out the door toward the car to be the first to hug her son,. She was in full of joy. I said hello you are still my best girl. Inside the house were my family, friends, and some neighbors. It seemed like everyone wanted to see me and I didn't know why. I went into some distant place in my mind and said hello to everyone and asked my mother if I could just go to my room. She walked me up to my room and I went into it and said I was tired. I'll see you all later. I could hear the talk downstairs and everyone seemed to just disappear. My brothers and sisters wanted to come into my room to see me and talk about the war but the door was locked. I could hear my mother saying just let him rest. Two days went by before I knew it and my mother knocked on the door, I opened it and let her in. She sat on the edge of the bed next to me and said everything is going to be all right. It will just take some time. I was setting my stereo up in my room when my father came in and heard jazz music from Archie Shepp and John Coltrane playing. He said I didn't know you liked jazz, dad smiled and talked about how he used to play saxophone with the Canton Spirituals as a boy back in Canton, Mississippi before World War II. He left the room saying glad you're here son. I asked my baby brother what was dad doing while I was in Vietnam. My brother said he never said much but everyday would come home from work and ask my mother was there a letter from "James." My mother would sit in her room silently and sometimes my father would close their door so others wouldn't see her cry. I tried avoiding talking about the war with the family and stayed in my room all day and night. There were telephone calls all day and sometimes at night from relatives, friends and neighbors asking about me. My mother would answer them and say I was doing fine and looked well. He will call you when he's up to it. About a week went by before my cousin who served in Vietnam with me and we had seen each other over there one time at the beginning of my tour came to my house. He had returned nine months before I was to come home. I remembered the visit to his post at Quin Oin, Vietnam. He was "short" meaning 30 days and a wake up in military language. He told everyone in the barracks that we were cousins and who would believe two first cousins would be in the same place fighting a war. My cousin talked about a Vietcong sniper who was killing soldiers everyday by picking them off on the way to the mess hall. He said the men went on patrol but were not able to find him. Most of the soldiers were nervous when they got close to going home that this ghost sniper was going to kill them instead of making it out of Vietnam. Andrew was excited that we were both home. He asked about Shirley and Booker. I guess he was too nervous to admit that we were not the same. My cousin had married his girlfriend from high school and had his own apartment in the Cabrini Green projects. He wanted me to come over and see the place. I never came. As the days went by I looked into college placement magazines and decided to go to Southern Illinois University Carbondale, Illinois. Since my application came back with a military scholarship and no tuition fees required. My second brother was already at Northwestern University and getting ready for Medical School at Washington University. Everyone in the neighborhood was talking about how proud they were of him becoming a doctor from the ghetto. He had graduated from Lane Tech High School and now Northwestern College with a Biology degree in the top of his dass. I was proud of him and tried to tell him that. He was leaving first and we all were excited but on his way out the door of the house he turned around and said my brother who served in Vietnam is the greatest hero of all times and I will never stop talking about him as my hero. I was stunned and never said a word. My dad with tears in his eyes just stood at the foot of the stairs and watched me go to my room and close the door. The letter came for me overnight to enter Southern Illinois University in the fall of 1971. The house seemed happy and excited again. My sister had been admitted to the University of Illinois and another sister to De Paul University. It looked like my mothers dreams and predictions were becoming a reality. She was overjoyed with her children. I remember getting ready to leave for college and how the house again went silent as it did the day I left for Vietnam. My mother was bragging about her children all over the house. My younger brothers were practicing with the band they created called "Soulful Children" and my dad was silent. When I came down stairs my father and mother were both at the door and seemed to want me not leave but keep me with them forever. I told them I will see you in a week. Dad walked to the taxi cab as I was leaving and the driver said the ride to the bus station was free to a war hero. My dad said I'll see you sergeant. I was never to live in that house again.

College was a strange place to me with students from all over the world on campus. It seemed like another Vietnam at first. I stayed to myself in the dorm room and my roommate was from East St Louis. He was the son of two college teachers in an East St Louis Jr. College. Lee and I would be best friends for the four years. He was a fraternity member and talked about Alpha Phi Alpha fraternity as the group to belong with since his father was an Alpha. He was going to be a lawyer. I remembered how my father once said my son will be a lawyer and a senator one day. I just smiled and kept the thoughts to myself. Lee convinced me to become an Alpha pledge. And all the brothers had found out about me serving in Vietnam and wanted to hear stories about the war. I said it was hell and lets just forget about it. They never stopped talking about it behind my back and some even talked about the picture of me that appeared in a Chicago paper as a war hero. This was all over the campus so I hid behind sunglasses and never talked about the war.

Once I went home with Lee and met his parents, they knew all about me through lee and his father said I'm honored to meet you. On my first visit to their home he said I understand son why you won't talk about the war. Lee's family friends gathered to meet me and lee said we were in a hurry to get back to campus because it was finals week. He protected me against that crowd. Back on campus things were not going as expected. I struggled through classes and realized something was missing. I didn't have the energy to compete at the level needed to become a lawyer. The war had taken it its toll on my talents. Hanging in the school of social welfare I was able to get through undergraduate work and wondered where will I go once I leave college. My brother was at Washington University Medical School and doing well. He was destined to become a doctor. I didn't see my future so I started searching college placement job listings for a future. I sent out 500 resumes during my senior year and one day close to graduation I got a call to the university presidents office. I thought it was more bad news. In the office were two businessmen waiting to see me. I thought they were from the CIA. The president came out and said I want you to talk with them about a job. They were from the pharmaceutical industry. I was offered a job in St. Louis, Missouri with a new car, expense account, salary, and even arranged housing. It seemed like a dream. I asked, why me? The men told me they knew the university president and he said you are a war hero and served above and beyond the call of duty. We think you are an asset the university and your country so we'd be honored to have you with us. The day after graduation they came in the new car and drove me to St. Louis, Missouri. I was put up in a top-flight hotel with all expenses paid and left with the car and expense account. The new district manager stated that we would look for a place for me while in the field working. He took me to a set of condominiums in Paddock Forest, MO and said I think you'll like it here. This place was surrounded with a swimming pool, clubhouse, corvettes, and jaguar cars in front of each condominium. I was given the place next door to an independent and single African American businessman. The company had printed my picture in its newspaper and sent copies to my family members, university, and neighborhood friends back home about the success of this Vietnam veteran. My mother came to visit with my younger brothers and she was overwhelmed by what she saw. I told her she would have everything she ever wanted once I made a success out of this new career. I had sent home half of my check every month while in the service and the insurance was in her name if I didn't make it out of Vietnam. She never stopped saying this is my boy and my favorite son. I think she was just happy that my life was going the way it was. The district manager had served in the navy and World War II and he had told my mother that your son is a hero and we are glad to have him on board.

This career would last 15 years before turning another chapter in my life. I achieved several milestones in the pharmaceutical industry. I was district distinguished sales representative and regional sales representative in less than five years. I came home to Chicago and had to hide in my mother's house to avoid cheering crowds in the ghetto neighborhood and was introduced to my wife to be by my cousin. It was the younger sister of his wife. Little did I know he was going to be divorced the year after we were married because of alcohol and drugs he was using to forget the Vietnam war.

My brother graduated from medical school during my first year with the company, second in his class. My mother was at the graduation and saw this . He said in his valedictorian speech that my mother is the greatest in all the world and she should be standing there instead of him. He married a nurse during his internship and always talked about his brother the war hero. Just as I was getting settled in my career and planning to buy my mother and dad a house in St Louis, I got the news that my father was sick and to come home. I hurried and he passed away two days after I got home. I buried my father with a picture of me in a foxhole during an attack in Phan Rhang Vietnam in April 1969. It was in his shirt pocket next to his heart. I knew my father would understand that he was a real soldier who will never be forgotten. There was fighting among us siblings who were out of college as to who gets my mother. She sat quietly during discussions and finally said I want to go with my favorite son the other soldier. I was preparing to get a house for her and my younger siblings when the news came that my mother had passed away. I was devastated and thought my whole world had perished. The war, my father, and now my best girl. Her funeral brought another change in my life and the siblings that words could never explain.

My youngest bother went with me and my new wife. The remaining siblings all went with relatives and boyfriends. We were never to be the same again. I left the pharmaceutical industry due to downsizing and returned back to Illinois to work for the state department of children and family services as a social worker. My youngest brother never got over my mother's death and along with a seizure disorder he died before his 21st birthday from a seizure. I had my wife and two children to keep me company in such a bad time. It seemed as though I was fighting on two fronts all the time. I wanted a successful career but Vietnam and the deaths of my loved ones continued to create a struggle proving my mother was right that all her children would succeed regardless of race, poverty, or lack of support. The soldier in me was fighting memories of death, destruction, and love of family. It was taking its toll on my family and my wife separated from me with the children. I was on a spiral going nowhere but down. I lost my job for absenteeism and seemed to be unable to work anywhere for failure to be consistent in coming into work. The alcohol and drugs seemed to control my life at this time and I landed in the Veterans Hospital on a suicide attempt in 1991. This was the first of three trips. On the second trip again nothing seemed to matter and I left the hospital to live in a shelter called Last Call Ministry. In there I found salvation. There were men who experience the Vietnam War, ghetto, and loss of family members with experiences that resulted in a worse condition than mine but they were alive. I went out of the shelter and started to struggle back to getting on my feet. I landed a job with the private sector of DCFS and was doing fine until I was going to work one day and started hearing helicopters and M-16 bullets coming out of the skies. I didn't know what was wrong and I ran home to be secluded in my room locked away with alcohol and drugs for two weeks. Someone came to my place Saturday from Last Call and a church. They convinced me to go back to the Veterans Hospital. At the hospital for the third time it seemed hopeless until a doctor came into the room one day and said you know why you're having this struggle? I said of course not. He said you're still fighting the war and its over, you just have to learn to live with it. This was the beginning of a new peace in my life for the first time since high school. I left the VA with referrals to PTSD groups and outpatient treatment organizations like the American Legion, Disabled Veterans, Paralyzed Veterans, Wounded

Warriors, and Blinded Veterans came to my support. I began to realize that I was not alone. I was unable to get my marriage back but a good relationship between my two kids and my wife still exists down through the years.

In 1996 I was able to go on vacation to Jerusalem, Israel. This was an exciting time since it is the Holy Land. I saw the birth and burial places of Jesus Christ. The Jordan River, the Wailing Wall, Massada Desert, and numerous other historical sights. The question about faith came up over and over again. I told a Jewish elder at the synagogue that my faith came on the battlefields of Vietnam. This was a turning point into who I would be for the rest of my life. I would be sergeant Willis, a soldier until I die. A soldier for Christ in a lifetime of humanitarian work. While working in the system I met several interesting African American veterans from World War 11 and Vietnam. There was one story from Iraq and Afghanistan; all of these are worthy of sharing with you in the struggle. I asked a World War II veteran what it was like serving in Germany during the war. He said the African American soldiers were assigned to the rear at all times. Up in the Rhine River where Hitler's troops were you could see from the rear at times. The African American troops did all of the meaningless jobs. He was a truck driver and on one occasion a general came into the rear and saw all the black troops sitting around doing meaningless tasks. He told the captain that all the truck drivers were to drive supplies to the front line troops (whites) down a mined road and not to go any less than 60 miles an hour in the midnight. The truck he was assigned with his buddy was flying down the road when his partner jumped off. He said I was afraid when I got to the front that I was going to have to explain why he jumped out to an all white officer group. When he got to the top of the hill, the buddy soldier was already in camp waiting for him. Fear of dying in a minefield can do strange things to a person. A Vietnam Veteran who was an African American serving as a lieutenant told a story how he was treated as the only black officer in a platoon with white soldiers. He said all the dirty and dangerous assignments were given to him by a racist captain. He said everyone knew the captain was trying to get him killed because he was a black officer. He survived the tour in Vietnam but got no recognition for bravery in the face of the enemy. An African American who served in Iraq told the story of how a group of soldiers banded together by race only in combat action. He said it was all about recognition for white soldiers and just getting back home for African Americans.

These stories and many others continue to haunt my life and the struggle every black man sees in this America. I reflect on the ministry work I was called upon to do by our Lord and Savior Jesus Christ and how it started in the streets of Chicago, Cook County Jail, Stroger's Hospital, and various nursery homes after becoming licensed through Last Call Ministry and the Church of God in Christ. Elder Ford and Elder Booker were the most influential on my life with their exceptional lives as ministers. My elder brother Ron Cummings will never be forgotten and I must tell the story he once gave about how he was a Beautician for years and made a lot of money until drugs and alcohol caught up with him and he found himself dying in an alley one February morning all alone. He fell during the night on his way home and spent the night in the freezing alley. A passerby in the street saw him lying there in the alley and called for help. If this person sent by God had not come by the story would never have been told. Ron started Last Call Ministry in 1987 and I worked as a volunteer counselor and social worker in the ministry from 1995 to 2010 when it was closed for lack of financial assistance. The struggle of every black man continues in the lives of people who need help the most. Working in the shelter system of Chicago from 1999 through 2008 as a clinical therapist for Beacon Therapeutic I was able to experience so many situations in which my college education, ministry work, and military experiences were put to use in order to help people who were hurting and struggling. There were so many homeless families it looked like the system never intended to help the poor and struggling black families. I remember several stories in which my gifts were able to reach out and assist. The ones that stand out the most are as follows: a 30-year-old African American male with his wife and five kids were in a shelter that I was assigned and he told me during the clinical assessment that he was once a member of a gang. He said that his grandmother raised him since both parents died from drugs when he was a small child. He grew up hanging out in the streets of Chicago and this caused his affiliation with the gang. His grandmother was a praying woman and never gave up hope on him. The crowd that he ran with was a tough one and his best friend was feared in the streets. One day as the two were leaving a building the friend turned and went right out of the doorway. As he was going to follow he heard his grandmothers voice saying go left. He went left and immediately heard 12 shots to the right. His friend was dead and he was alive. He believed his grandmother's prayers saved his life and that was the change which made him realize what was most important in life. He said I don't have very much economically but I have my wife and kids. The wife stated he was a good husband and the kids all love him. This change was most important in him as a person that his grandmother's prayers. He said that I was being told his story because I reminded him of his grandmother.

I remembered one more story from an original member of the Tuskegee Airmen who was a fighter pilot in World War II. He spoke on his last mission in Germany. The captain told me that just as he went over the Rhine River in the war the plane was shot down and he bailed out. He was certain that he would be dead before he hit the ground, but as he got closer to the ground, a crowd had gathered of German people and they all seemed to be clapping. He thought they were happy because he had been shot down and would be captured. As he landed on the ground he heard the talking and since he spoke some German he understood them to be excited because they thought it was a circus act that Hitler had ordered. They had no idea that a black man could fly an F100 or any plane. He was taken to prison by a battalion of German soldiers because they were watching the plane go down from 10 miles away and followed the smoke. He did say that while in captivity he was treated as an officer by the German soldiers but would not talk about the day-to-day activity. He stayed in captivity until the end of the war. The struggle goes on and on and America just watches.

www.ingramcontent.com/pod-product-compliance
Lightning Source LLC
Chambersburg PA
CBHW031302120626
46545CB00007B/2944